PUT YOUR FAVORITE PHOTO HERE!

THE JOY of Children

TYNDALE HOUSE PUBLISHERS, INC.

WHEATON, ILLINOIS

Visit Tyndale's exciting Web site at www.tyndale.com

Development Director Tammy Faxel

Designed by Gloria Keibler

Edited by Erin Keeley

Table of contents

Introduction

Oh, the joy of children! There's nothing like watching the delight on a child's face while he or she smells a flower (even if, to you, it's just a dandelion). Or enjoying their playful skipping down the sidewalk on a sunny day—or their wild stomping in mud puddles on a rainy one.

Children have the awesome ability to infuse our souls with joy. Everything they see is new, exciting, and wondrous. And whether you're a parent, grandparent, teacher, aunt or uncle, or someone who just loves children, you have a marvelous opportunity to watch, listen, and learn from these little ones.

The Joy of Children allows you to celebrate life through a child's eyes. With sections on Home Sweet Home, Simple Joys, Togetherness, Celebration, Growing Up, Laughter, Friendship, Love, Learning Together, and Memories, this book is filled with art by children, quotes, verses, and prayers. Personalize your book by adding photos and recording your thoughts in the designated spaces. And don't forget to try the simple activities in "Activities with Children." When you do, you'll be sure to get a smile and a hug from the children you spend time with.

Home sweet home—how that

Home sweet home

home sweet home—how that phrase warms the heart! Whether you live in a house, condo, town house, or apartment, there's nothing more wonderful and restful than coming home to your very own place. It doesn't matter whether it's one hundred years old or only a few because it reflects you and your family—your style, tastes, and individuality.

Home is also the place where you can share conversations, concerns, tears, and laughter with those you care about most.

For better and for worse, home is the dwelling where, as Robert Frost wrote, "When you have to go there, they have to take you in!" No wonder it's thought of as home sweet home—because it's a place where each family member should feel unconditional acceptance and love.

And in being "sweet," a home also has tremendous opportunities to be "pleasing to the senses": the sounds of gentle laughter, bedtime stories being read, and the quiet creaking of a rocking chair; the sights of glowing candles on the dinner table after a long day of work; the taste of freshly baked cookies after school, homemade applesauce in the fall, and lemonade in the summer; the smells of baby powder and familiar perfume; and the touch of hands joined for mealtime prayers.

"Home" means it's a place full of beginnings: birthdays, newborn pups, carefully planted seeds, easy-reader books, training wheels, and piano lessons. It's a place where prayers are said throughout a long night until a fever breaks; a place where forgiveness is pursued after confessions of wrongdoings; a place where superglue is used to rescue broken dishes, and where hugs and prayers for a prodigal child last long after the tears subside.

No matter how temporary or permanent your "home" is, it has great possibilities to be a place of growth, love, and security for the children in your life.

Madeline, 6

We are God's household, if we keep up our courage and
remain confident in our hope in Christ.

HEBREWS 3:6

Activities with Children

1

Spend some cozy time at home with a special child in your life.

Listen to your favorite CD together.

2

Ask an appliance store for an empty refrigerator box. They are usually free for the asking.

You can create a castle, playhouse, submarine, or rocket. The possibilities are endless!

Antics & Anecdotes

FUNNY THINGS CHILDREN SAY AND DO . . .

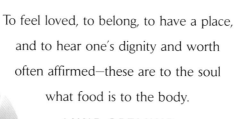

To feel loved, to belong, to have a place,
and to hear one's dignity and worth
often affirmed—these are to the soul
what food is to the body.

ANNE ORTLUND

put my picture here!

A house is built by wisdom and becomes strong through good sense. Through knowledge its rooms are filled with all sorts of precious riches and valuables.

PROVERBS 24:3-4

11

A house is built by human hands, but a home is built by human hearts.

ANONYMOUS

Christina, 11

Thoughts and Prayers

Life is richest when a person discovers true peace and joy at home. May your home be blessed with a serenity to withstand the major and minor crises that touch your doorstep.

PRAYER

Lord, let my home be a haven of security and peace for the children who pass through its doors. May the conversations that take place within these walls be pleasing to you and encouraging to others. Thank you for the gift of home. Amen.

THOUGHTS ABOUT HOME

Children enjoy

Simple joys

life's simple joys. . . .

*C*hildren enjoy life's simple joys—those things that are available, spontaneous, and pure. These joys are captured in natural packages, such as flowers, ladybugs, and skipping in the rain, and unfold as treasures that delight hearts of all ages.

When we witness a child's first tottering steps or hear an older child read a favorite book, imitating our inflections, the pressures of meetings, bills, and phone calls grow properly dim. In the midst of difficult stages (the two-year-old whose favorite word is *no!*), frantic schedules, and daily demands, children remind us of what is truly valuable, precious, and long lasting.

Kelsey, 7

Children call us to cherish the moment. As author Henri Nouwen says, "Children always challenge me to live in the present. They want me to be with them here and now, and they find it hard to understand that I might have other things to do or think about." Children refresh us with surprises—pointing out a rainbow with a chubby finger, losing a tooth in a peanut-butter sandwich, gleefully splashing during bath time. They encourage us to catch snowflakes with our tongues.

As we learn about simple joys through a child's eyes, we also discover that sometimes setting aside the task at hand reaps a sweet

reward: a hug or a graham-cracker-crumb kiss. Children teach us how to relax, how to share life through smiling, holding hands, eating ice-cream cones, catching fish, shopping for bargains, creating homemade cards, playing games, and watching a fuzzy caterpillar wiggle through the grass.

These invaluable reminders are surely gifts from heaven's hand and heart, given to us for our refreshment, relaxation, and restoration. Thank God for simple joys!

Taneisha, 7

Every good and perfect gift is from above,

coming down from the Father of the heavenly lights.

JAMES 1:17, NIV

Activities with Children

1

Camp out in the kitchen. On a rainy or cold day, put a sheet over the kitchen table

and a blanket on the floor. Play "camping" together in your homemade tent.

2

Prepare a box of instant pudding as directed. Pour a small amount of pudding on a large

piece of waxed paper. With your fingers, draw pictures and write your names in the pudding.

Don't worry about the mess. Just have fun doing something different.

Antics & Anecdotes

FUNNY THINGS CHILDREN SAY AND DO . . .

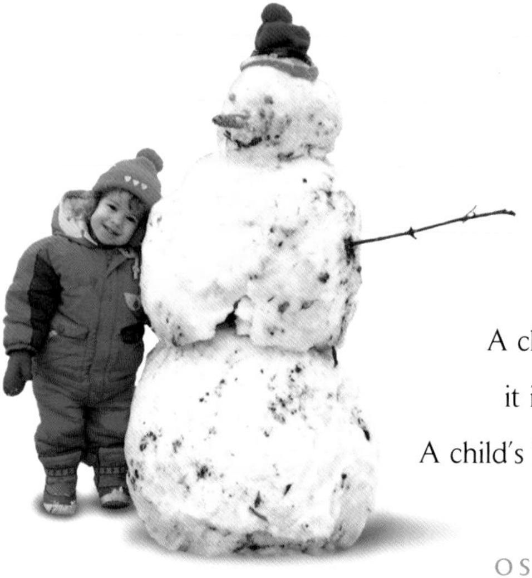

A child's life has not dates,
it is free, silent, dateless.
A child's life ought to be a child's life,
full of simplicity.

OSWALD CHAMBERS

put my picture here!

This is the day the Lord has made. We will rejoice and be glad in it.

PSALM 118:24

The cardboard box is marked "The Good Stuff." As I write, I can see where it is stored on a high shelf in my studio. I like being able to see it when I look up. The box contains those odds and ends of personal treasures that have survived many bouts of clean-it-out-and-throw-it-away that seize me from time to time. It has passed through the screening done as I've moved from house to house and hauled stuff from attic to attic. A thief looking into the box would not take anything. But if the house ever catches on fire, the box goes with

Melanie, 7

me when I run.

One of the keepsakes in the box is a small paper bag. Lunch size. Though the top is sealed with duct tape, staples, and several paper clips, there is a ragged rip in one side through which the contents may be seen.

This particular lunch sack has been in my care for maybe fourteen years. But it really belongs to my daughter, Molly. Soon after she came of school age, she became an enthusiastic

participant in packing lunches for herself, her brothers, and me. Each bag got a share of sandwiches, apples, milk money, and sometimes a note or a treat. One morning, Molly handed me two bags. One regular lunch sack. And the other one with the duct tape and staples and paper clips.

"Why two bags?"

"The other one is something else."

"What's in it?"

"Just some stuff—take it with you."

Not wanting to hold court over the matter, I stuffed both sacks into my briefcase, kissed the child, and rushed off.

At midday, while hurriedly scarfing down my real lunch, I tore open Molly's bag and shook out the contents. Two hair ribbons, three small stones, a plastic dinosaur, a pencil stub, a tiny seashell, two animal crackers, a marble, a used lipstick, a small doll, two chocolate kisses, and thirteen pennies.

I smiled. How charming. Rising to hustle off to all the important business of the after-noon, I swept the desk clean, into the wastebasket—leftover lunch, Molly's junk and all. There wasn't anything in there I needed.

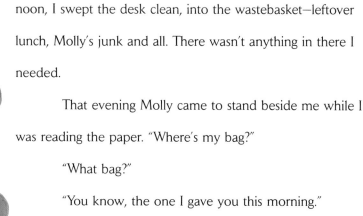

Christina, 11

That evening Molly came to stand beside me while I was reading the paper. "Where's my bag?"

"What bag?"

"You know, the one I gave you this morning."

"I left it at the office, why?"

"I forgot to put this note in it." She handed over the note. "Besides, I want it back."

"Why?"

"Those are my things in the sack, Daddy, the ones I really like. I thought you might like to play with them, but now I want them back. You didn't lose the bag, did you, Daddy?" Tears puddled in her eyes.

"Oh, no. I just forgot to bring it home," I lied.

"Bring it tomorrow. OK?"

"Sure thing—don't worry." As she hugged my neck with relief, I unfolded the note that had not gotten into the sack: "I love you, Daddy."

Oh. And also—uh-oh.

I looked long at the face of my child.

She was right—what was in that sack was "something else." Molly had given me her treasures. All that a seven-year-old held dear. Love in a paper sack. And I had missed it. Not

only missed it, but had thrown it away because "there wasn't anything in there I needed."

Dear God.

It wasn't the first or last time I felt my Daddy Permit was about to run out.

It was a long trip back to the office. But there was nothing else to be done. So I went. The pilgrimage of a penitent. Just ahead of the janitor. I picked up the wastebasket and poured the contents on my desk. I was sorting it all out when the janitor came in to do his chores.

"Lose something?"

"Yes, my mind."

"It's probably in there, all right. What's it look like, and I'll help you find it."

I started not to tell him. But I couldn't feel any more of a fool than I was already in fact, so I told him.

He didn't laugh. "I got kids too." So the brotherhood of fools searched the trash and found the jewels, and he smiled at me and I smiled at him. You are never alone in these things. Never.

After washing the mustard off the dinosaur and spraying the whole thing with breath freshener to kill the smell of onions, I carefully smoothed out the wadded ball of brown paper into a semifunctional bag and put the treasures inside and carried it home gingerly, like an injured kitten. The next evening, I returned it to Molly, no questions asked, no explanations offered. The bag didn't look so good, but the stuff was all there, and that's what counted.

Emily, 5

After dinner I asked her to tell me about the stuff in the sack, and so she took it all out one piece at a time and placed the objects in a row on the dining-room table. It took a long time to tell. Everything had a story, a memory, or was attached to dreams and imaginary friends. Fairies had brought some of the things. And I had given her the chocolate kisses, and she had kept them for when she needed them. I managed to say "I see" very wisely several times in the telling. And, as a matter of fact, I did see.

To my surprise, Molly gave the bag to me once again several days later. Same ratty bag. Same stuff inside. I felt forgiven. And trusted. And loved. And a little more comfortable wearing the title of Father. Over several months, the bag went with me from time to time. It was never clear to me why I did or did

not get it on a given day. I began to think of it as the Daddy Prize and tried to be good the night before so I might be given it the next morning.

In time Molly turned her attention to other things—found other treasures, lost interest in the game, grew up. Something. Me? I was left holding the bag. She gave it to me one morning and never asked for its return. And so I have it still.

Sometimes I think of all the times in this sweet life when I must have missed affection I was being given. A friend calls this "standing knee-deep in the river and dying of thirst."

So the worn paper sack is there in the box. Left from a time when a child said, "Here—this is the best I've got—take it—it's yours. Such as I have, give I to thee."

I missed the first time. But it's my bag now.

Enjoy the little things. One day you may look back
and realize they were the big things.

BETTY COMBS

Grace, 7

Thoughts and Prayers

Children have a natural gift for appreciating the simple things in life: crunching autumn leaves underfoot or making angels in the snow. Discover the joys of unhurried, simple pleasures with a child in your life.

PRAYER

Dear Lord, please help me recognize the abundant joy you offer. Help me to pass on this pure delight to the children in my life. Let them see in me the radiance that comes from knowing your peace, and help them to make you a part of their lives. Amen.

THOUGHTS ABOUT SIMPLE JOYS

What does it mean

Togetherness

to be truly "together"? . . .

love being with you. I love it when we're together." We long to hear those words from people who are important to us! From birth through the seasons of life, we all need to feel a sense of belonging, of "togetherness." When you picnic with your family or friends, when you throw a party for a child's birthday, you're celebrating that togetherness.

What does it mean to be truly "together"? The very word implies the warmth of a relationship: a mother to a daughter, a friend to a neighbor or coworker, a grandparent to a grandson. Fun times of building snowmen, snuggling on snowy days, and kissing each other good-bye are anchors to hang on to throughout life. Togetherness means you enjoy cooperating—and that brings contentment to your soul. Mundane tasks such as raking leaves, weeding the garden, and folding laundry become treasured memories of times spent with those you love.

Being together isn't always easy . . . like when flu germs are passed, when dirty dishes are piling up, when the six kids in your play group are all getting on each other's nerves, when someone is monopolizing the bathroom. That's when loyalty comes into play— a loyalty that expands the boundaries of location, age, position, and little annoyances.

God created togetherness when he designed families. Heredity, adoption, and friendship are all ways families can be created. Birthdays and holidays provide

Kathryn, 7

37

wonderful opportunities for "families" to gather and celebrate. Smaller events such as a football game on TV or a visit from a long-distance

treasured friend can be more spontaneous times of togetherness. With children, togetherness might imply bedtime routines of a bath and a favorite book, Lego construction projects, bread-baking days, romps in the woods, visits to the doctor, and camping trips.

But just planning events doesn't guarantee the warm spirit of togetherness. It must be nurtured through time, love, and loyalty—much like plants must be cared for, watered, and fed. Then the group will harvest the results "together" with joy!

Ian, 9

Love each other with genuine affection,

and take delight in honoring each other.

ROMANS 12:10

Activities with Children

1

Take a penny walk. At every corner toss a penny.

Heads means you turn right; tails means you turn left.

Go home and drink a cup of warm cocoa or apple cider together.

2

Collect empty paper-towel tubes and several small boxes.

Make "robots" from these materials.

Antics & Anecdotes

FUNNY THINGS CHILDREN SAY AND DO . . .

If you want your children
to turn out well,
spend twice as much time with them,
and half as much money.

ABIGAIL VAN BUREN

put my picture here!

So encourage each other and build each other up,

just as you are already doing.

1 THESSALONIANS 5:11

n 1989 an 8.2 earthquake flattened Armenia, killing over thirty thousand people in less than four minutes.

In the midst of utter devastation and chaos, a father left his wife securely at home and rushed to the school where his son was supposed to be, only to discover that the building was as flat as a pancake.

After the traumatic initial shock, he remembered the promise he had made to his son: "No matter what, I'll always be there for you!" And the tears began to fill his eyes. As he looked at the pile of debris that once was the school, it looked hopeless, but he kept remembering his commitment to his son.

He began to concentrate on where he walked his son to class at school each morning. Remembering his son's classroom would be in the back right corner of the building, he rushed there and started digging through the rubble.

As he was digging,

other forlorn parents arrived, clutching their hearts, saying, "My son!" "My daughter!" Other well-meaning parents tried to pull him off of what was left of the school, saying:

"It's too late!"

"They're dead!"

"You can't help!"

"Go home!"

"Come on, face reality; there's nothing you can do!"

"You're just going to make things worse!"

To each parent he responded with one line: "Are you going to help me now?" And then he proceeded to dig for his son, stone by stone.

The fire chief showed up and tried to pull him off of the school's debris, saying, "Fires are breaking out; explosions are happening everywhere. You're in danger. We'll take care of it. Go home." To which this loving, caring Armenian father asked, "Are you going to help me now?"

The police came and said, "You're angry, distraught, and it's over. You're endangering others. Go home. We'll handle it!" To which he replied, "Are you going to help me now?" No one helped.

Courageously he proceeded alone because he needed to know for himself: "Is my boy alive or is he dead?"

He dug for eight hours . . . twelve hours . . . twenty-four hours . . . thirty-six hours . . . then, in the thirty-eighth hour, he pulled back a boulder and heard his son's voice. He screamed his son's name, "Armand!"

Kelsey, 7

He heard back, "Dad?! It's me, Dad! . . . You promised, `No matter what, I'll always be there for you!' You did it, Dad! . . . No matter what, I know you'll be there for me!"

47

If a child is to keep alive his inborn sense of wonder,

he needs the companionship of at least

one adult who can share it, rediscovering with him the joy,

excitement and mystery of the world we live in.

RACHEL CARSON

Kathryn, 7

Thoughts and Prayers

Time together doesn't occur automatically in our fast-paced world—we have to plan for it and make it happen. And if it's truly important to us, we will! We create time to be with those we love—first.

Lord, please bless the children in my life with a solid family structure. Give them times of wonderful togetherness to cherish for the rest of their lives. Let them know the security of belonging. Amen.

THOUGHTS ABOUT TOGETHERNESS

How do you celebrate? . . . .

Celebration

how do you celebrate? With brightly patterned packages with bows? A special cake? Streamers and colorful balloons? A beautiful floral arrangement? Surprise deliveries? A meaningful card?

There are hundreds of occasions to celebrate—birthdays, anniversaries, graduations, and promotions, for starters. Then there are the traditional holidays when we share family recipes, gifts, cards, and reflective joy: Christmas, Thanksgiving, New Year's, and Easter.

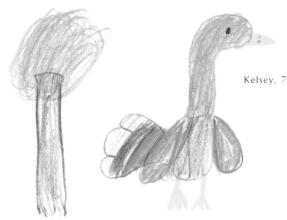

Kelsey, 7

The idea of celebration is not new;
it's been around for myriad centuries. In fact, the
Bible itself talks of historic Jewish festivals with
rites and rituals and comments on the changing
seasons. Mmm . . . how often have we thought of
celebrating the fact that fall or spring has arrived?

There are *so* many things to celebrate—and traditional days are
only the beginning. Some of life's most worthy celebrations are really
the smallest of occasions. They may be defined by a day, a conversa-
tion, a particular decision, or a prayer of trust. But they are marked by
their depth of meaning, the intimacy of the relationship, and the

authenticity of heart. How can we take advantage of these precious moments?

Each time a child takes a first step, we can offer heartfelt praise. We can share mutual excitement when a tooth loosens or when a child accomplishes toilet training. We can share a hug as a child goes off to his or her first day at school. We can record special conversations in our journal for future reflection. We can laugh together over bath-time play. We can walk through the park, holding a little one's hand, and thank God for his precious gift of life.

Each day, no matter how quiet or rushed, is full of celebratory moments. So look for a joyous reason to celebrate!

Kathryn, 7

Melanie, 7

Celebrate because of all the good things the Lord your God

has given to you and your household.

DEUTERONOMY 26:11

Activities with Children

1

Make cards together for those special people in your lives.

Don't forget each other!

2

Celebrate a young child's first bicycle ride without training wheels, first day of school,

or first tooth lost. Celebrate an older child's sporting event, music recital, or first paycheck.

Antics & Anecdotes

It isn't the great big pleasures that count the most;

it's making a great deal out of the little ones.

JEAN WEBSTER

put my picture here!

It is the Lord your God who gives you bountiful harvests and blesses all your work.

This festival will be a time of great joy for all.

DEUTERONOMY 16:15

olly was a dear girl who lived long ago on a large farm with plenty of chickens, cows, and horses; but Polly never thought much about how nice all these were, for her father and mother were always hard at work. The two brothers worked with their father; her sister helped her mother in the house; and Polly washed the dishes, scoured the knives, fed the chickens, and ran errands for the family and for all the summer boarders besides.

One of the boarders, Miss Cary, was watching Polly shell peas one morning and thinking that she did a great deal of work for such a little girl. Finally she asked, "How old are you, Polly?"

"Eight," Polly answered.

"You're almost nine," said her mother.

"When is her birthday?" asked Miss Cary.

"Why, let me see; it's this month sometime—the seventeenth of July. I declare, I'd have forgotten all about it if you hadn't spoken." And Mrs. Jones went on with her work again.

"What's a birthday?" Polly asked shyly.

"Why, Polly," exclaimed Miss Cary, "don't you know? It's the anniversary of the day you were born. Didn't you ever have a birthday present, Polly?"

"No," said Polly, looking puzzled.

"We never have much time for these things," Polly's mother said. "It's about all I can do to remember Christmas."

"Yes, I know," Miss Cary said, but she resolved that Polly should have a birthday.

When she came down to breakfast the morning of the seventeenth, Miss Cary met

Polly in the hall and, putting a little purse into her hand, said kindly, "Here, Polly, is something for you to buy birthday presents with."

Polly opened the little bag and found in it nine bright silver quarters. She ran as fast as she could to tell her mother.

"Why, child!" her mother said, "that's too much money for you to spend. Better save it. It will help buy you a pair of shoes and a warm dress next winter."

Almost any girl would have cried at this, and Polly's eyes did fill with tears; but as her mother wanted her to help "put the breakfast on," she took the plate of muffins into the dining room.

Bobbie, 7

Miss Cary noticed the wet lashes and said, "Mrs. Jones, please let Polly go down to the stores today and spend her birthday money."

Mrs. Jones could not refuse this request. So after she had put the baby to sleep, Polly was allowed to go down to the village, which was a good two miles away, all by herself. The happy girl would have willingly walked five miles to spend her precious money.

It was late in the afternoon when she came back. The boarders were lounging about, waiting for the supper bell to ring. They all smiled at the little figure toiling up the road, with her arms full of bundles.

Polly smiled back radiantly through the dust that covered her round little face as she called to Miss Cary, "Oh, I've got lots of things! Please come into the kitchen and see."

"No, it's too warm there," Miss Cary said. "Come into the living room, where it's cool, and we can all see."

So they went into the house, and Polly began to unwrap her packages and exhibit her purchases.

"There," she said as she tore the paper from an odd-shaped bundle. "This is for Mother"—she held up an eggbeater—"'cause it takes so long to beat eggs with a fork."

The boarders looked at each other in surprise, but Polly was too busy to notice.

She fairly beamed as she held up a green glass necktie pin for inspection. "Isn't it lovely?" she said. "It's for Father."

"This isn't much," she continued, opening a small bundle, "only a rattle for Baby. It cost five cents."

The boarders looked on in silence as the busy little fingers untied strings. No one knew whether to laugh or feel sorry.

It was wonderful what nine quarters would buy, and not strange that the little girl

Lindy, 5

had spent a whole half day shopping. There was a blue tie for brother Dan, and a pink one for Tim; a yellow hair ribbon for sister Linda; some hairpins for Grandma; and a small bottle of cologne for Jake, the "hired man." Then there was but one package left. Polly patted this lovingly as she opened it.

"This is the nicest of all, and it's for you," she said as she handed Miss Cary a box of pink writing paper. "It seemed too bad that you only had plain white paper to write on, when you write so lovely. So I got you this. Isn't it pretty?"

"Why, it's beautiful, Polly dear," Miss Cary said, "but what have you bought for your birthday present?"

"Why, these," said Polly, "these are all my presents. Presents are something we give away, aren't they?" And Polly looked around, wondering why all were so still.

"It is more blessed to give than to receive," said one of the boarders softly, and Miss Cary put her arms around Polly and kissed the hot, dusty little face again and again.

"It's been a lovely day," Polly said. "I never had any presents to give away before, and I think birthdays are just lovely."

The next month, after Miss Cary returned to the city, *she* had a birthday; and there

came to Polly a most wonderful doll, with beautiful clothes,
and a card saying, "For Polly,
on my birthday, from Lena
Cary," which, by the way,
immediately became the doll's
name.

Miss Cary was not
the only one who caught
Polly's idea of a birthday. The
rest of the boarders remem-
bered, and through the year, as each one's birthday came, Polly received a gift to delight her
generous little heart.

When the seventeenth of July came around again, Miss Cary was not on the farm,
but she sent Polly a little silk bag with ten silver quarters in it—and Polly still thinks "birthdays
are lovely."

You don't have to wait for a birthday to have fun.

You can create your own celebrations.

ALEXANDRA STODDARD

Christina, 11

Thoughts and Prayers

From homemade waffles on Saturday mornings to bedtime prayers each night, it is often the small traditions that mean the most. Develop an awareness of the many ways you can make each day a celebration for those you love.

PRAYER

Help me, God, to share my celebrations with the young people in my life. Fill their lives with countless blessings to celebrate. And let them know those gifts are from you. Amen.

THOUGHTS ABOUT CELEBRATIONS

What did you want to be

Growing up

when you grew up? . . .

Christina, 11

What did you want to be when you grew up?

If you're like most people in the world, you probably changed your perspective many times. Maybe at four you wanted to be a beautician; at twelve you wanted to be a singer; at seventeen you wanted to be an accountant. And you might have changed your mind several times since then.

When booties are replaced with shoes, often children desire to be like those closest to them in their home. They want to walk like Dad or to talk like Mom. Then when snacks turn from animal crackers to

potato chips, often children desire to be their biggest hero—the one they most admire, such as a teacher, a movie star, a neighborhood fireman, a detective on TV. Then comes the time when easy-reader books are exchanged for CDs, tapes, and video games. That's

when children aspire to be like their friends. There's nothing more important to them than fitting in with their peer group. In essence, their "hero" becomes the friend who knows their deepest secrets and shares their biggest dreams.

Watching children grow up isn't always easy. It means that we witness their tumbles when they first begin to walk; we put up with

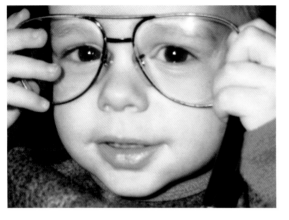

their two-year-old and teenage defiance. At times we take one step forward and two back with them. But as we provide guidance as children grow up, we can grow with them and learn more about life through their perspective as we watch them develop their unique talents.

When you think back over your own childhood, what people helped you in your growing-up years? What things did they do that impacted your life for the good? Just think—you have the marvelous opportunity to do the same things now for the children in *your* life!

Kelsey, 7

Molly, 10

And I am sure that God, who began the good work within you,

will continue his work until it is finally finished.

PHILIPPIANS 1:6

Activities with Children

1

Let your special child record his or her voice on a tape recorder. Have him or her mention

the weather today, favorite toys, and something special. Then play it back.

2

Dress up and serve dinner by candlelight.

It's a great time to teach children common courtesies and table manners.

Antics & Anecdotes

FUNNY THINGS CHILDREN SAY AND DO . . .

Children are not so different than kites. . . .

Children were created to fly.

But they need the wind—the undergirding and strength

that comes from unconditional love,

encouragement, and prayer.

GIGI GRAHAM TCHIVIDJIAN

put my picture here!

Don't make your children angry by the way you treat them.

Rather, bring them up with the discipline and instruction approved by the Lord.

EPHESIANS 6:4

Children are likely to live up to what you believe of them.

Chrissie, 7

Thoughts and Prayers

Children grow up before we know it! We have a limited amount of time to share our enthusiasm, love, and dreams with them, so make the most of each opportunity!

PRAYER

Dear Lord, please help the children I love to follow good examples, value character, and grow in compassion and respect for themselves and others. Thank you for your guidance in their lives. Amen.

THOUGHTS ABOUT GROWING UP

One of God's greatest gifts

Laughter

to humankind is laughter. . . .

G o ahead! Laugh it up!" Whoever coined the phrase for that bumper sticker had the right idea.

Truly one of God's greatest gifts to humankind is laughter. From a grandparent's deep chuckles to a preschooler's giggles, laughter enriches every heart. It eases the tension of a long week and increases our joy. A laughter-filled smile is universal in any language and can, indeed, make someone's day.

Of all the people in the world, children are the most spontaneous and natural laughers.

They love activities like tickle parties and games of hide-and-seek. Often they consider the chase the best part.

Kelly, 8

Mealtimes, too, create many opportunities for laughter. Children are wonderfully creative with food. Carrots can become whiskers, peas can become missiles perfect for throwing at an eagerly waiting dog, chocolate cake is a gooey texture made just for smearing over a child's face and hair. Messy? Yes—but these events will soon be only memories. When these things happen, go ahead—chuckle your way through those preschool years. Turn those snickers into laughter that can be enjoyed by all around the table.

A mispronounced word during story time or a funny face made while describing the day's events can lead to bedtime chuckles.

So enjoy those moments to the hilt—let that chuckle move to a giggle, and then to downright hilarity. It'll release your cares of the day and create a memorable and joyful moment for both you and your special child.

Humor is heavenly, so let's celebrate it—even in the midst of difficult, demanding days. Thank God for the relief and delight laughter can bring!

Emily, 5

God has brought me laughter!

All who hear about this will laugh with me.

GENESIS 21:6

Activities with Children

1

Have a smile contest. See who has the biggest smile.

Measure with a ruler.

2

Use toothpicks to roast miniature marshmallows over a candle together.

When we do fun things with children,

they will be more likely to listen to us about serious things.

Antics & Anecdotes

FUNNY THINGS CHILDREN SAY AND DO . . .

God is a God of laughter, as well as prayer . . .

a God of singing, as well as of tears.

God is at home in the play of His children.

He loves to hear us laugh.

PETER MARSHALL

put my picture here!

A glad heart makes a happy face.

PROVERBS 15:13

Kid Quips

"I know the three parts of an insect: the head, the thorax—and just like my brother's name—the *Adam*en."

Sarah, age 7

Cara, 8

As the church offering basket passed by one Sunday, Heather, age 9, asked her mother, "Can I pay the bill this week?"

"Grandmas have lots of ruffles [wrinkles] on their faces, and they give lots of love." *Jenna, age 5*

"I wish God would turn the heat down, 'cause it's hot out here!" *Lindy, age 5*

"If Santa doesn't give me a puppy, I will ask God. You can always count on him!" *Brittany, age 7*

When asked why she still sucks her thumb, four-year-old Anna pertly replied, "'Cause it fits."

Seven-year-old Brittany told her grandfather, "Grandfather, your ears are bigger than mine, you know!" Peter, age 5, added, "Yeah, and they still don't work!"

When asked to name some of the things beeswax is used for, six-year-old Curtis raised his hand and said, "To fix my mom's eyebrows."

Ryan, age 4, was studying a nature jar and explained it to his friend: "That used to be a caterpillar. Now he's all wrapped up in a *raccoon*."

Laughter is a way of communicating joy,

and joy is a net of love by which we can catch souls.

MOTHER TERESA

Christina, 11

Thoughts and Prayers

Laughter comes from within, the evidence of a happy heart and a positive outlook. This remarkable gift can change the atmosphere, offering hope and joy to everyone. Laughter makes a day complete!

PRAYER

Lord, help the children in my life to know the precious ache of laughing until their sides hurt. Create in them a joy that notices the fun in life, and give them the confident ability to laugh at themselves. Amen.

THOUGHTS ABOUT LAUGHTER

We all need friends. . . .

Friendship

*h*opscotch. Slumber parties. Lemonade stands. Shooting hoops in the driveway . . .

All of these childhood activities are more fully enjoyed among friends. We all need friends; they make our quality of life richer and more exciting. The blessings of friendship are too numerous to count. Conversations of lighthearted chitchat, intense debate, or heartfelt hopes and dreams are all valuable ways to get to know one another. Action-packed Saturdays at play and struggling together through daily schoolwork provide important opportunities to interact and learn more about life.

Proverbs 18:24 states that "a real friend sticks closer than a brother."

Jenna, 10

A real friend is a compassionate encourager, a gentle truth-teller, an enthusiastic cheerleader, and a personal counselor all in one. Where do those special friendships—the kind that last a lifetime—begin, and how are they built?

Friendship is a learned skill and an effective teacher of character traits needed throughout life. As children grow and change, their friendships adapt with them. Babies enter life oblivious to everything apart from their own immediate needs. With a few tears or sweet sounds, he or she communicates a growling tummy, a wet diaper, the need for sleep, or pure contentment. As they grow, they develop a greater awareness of special people in their life, whether they are family members, caregivers, or another child who may end up being a best friend somewhere down the path of life.

During the next few years, watch as their curiosity grows and their social awareness develops into true enjoyment of their peers' company. With enough positive modeling of genuine caring, a child can learn to be a good friend in return.

One of the most wonderful aspects of friendship is that it is not ruled by age. A caring grandparent, older sibling, or fun-loving baby-sitter can be a child's best friend, especially during the relational ups and downs children experience with others their own age.

How fortunate is the child whose favorite playmate today will become a lifelong friend to share memories and dreams, heartaches and joys, prayers and hopes! Thank God for friendship!

Emma, 7

Kelsey, 7

Dear friend, I am praying that all is well with you.

3 JOHN 1:2

Activities with Children

1

Buy a small photo album, and help a child you know collect snapshots of his or her friends.

The album can be kept in a special place in the child's room

to show that friends should be treasured.

2

Host a slumber party for a special child in your life; let him or her invite a friend or two.

Talk, eat popcorn, and watch a favorite movie together.

Antics & Anecdotes

FUNNY THINGS CHILDREN SAY AND DO . . .

Jenna, 10

Friendship . . . is the instrument
by which God reveals to each
the beauties of all the others.

C. S. LEWIS

put my picture here!

A friend is always loyal, and a brother is

born to help in time of need.

PROVERBS 17:17

little boy who was quiet and shy moved to a new neighborhood. His name was Steve. One day he came home from school and said, "You know what, Mom? Valentine's Day is coming, and I want to make a valentine for everyone in my class. I want them to know that I'm their friend." His mother's heart sank as she thought, *I wish he wouldn't do that.*

Every afternoon
she had watched
the children
coming home from
school, laughing
and hanging on to

each other—all except Steve. He always walked
behind them.

She decided to go along with his plans,
however, so glue and paper and crayons were
purchased, and for three weeks Steve painstak-
ingly made thirty-five valentines. When the day
came to deliver the cards, he was very excited.
He stacked those valentines under his arm and
ran out the door. His mother thought, *This is
going to be a tough day for Steve. I'll bake some*

Taneisha, 7

Bobbie, 7

cookies and have some milk ready for him when he comes home from school. Maybe that will help ease the pain, since he won't be getting many valentines.

That afternoon she had the warm cookies and the milk ready. She went over to the window, scratched a little of the frost off the glass, and looked out. Sure enough, here came the gang of children, laughing, with valentines tucked under their arms. And there was her Steve.

Although still behind the children, he was walking faster than usual, and she thought, *Bless his heart. He's ready to break into tears.* His

arms were empty. He didn't have a single valentine.

Steve came into the house, and his mother said, "Sweetheart, Mom has some warm cookies and milk for you, just sit down. . . ." But Steve's face was all aglow. He marched right by her, and all he could say was: "Not a one, not a single one. I didn't forget one. They all know I'm their friend."

Friendship is the greatest of worldly goods.

Certainly to me it is the chief happiness of life.

C. S. LEWIS

Taneisha, 7

Thoughts and Prayers

Friends enhance and enrich our lives in a lot of ways. The art of friendship is learned early in life, and its gifts sustain us over the years. May you and the children in your midst be blessed by the joys of true friendship!

PRAYER

Dear God, please provide deep, fun-loving, and loyal friendships for the children in my life. Use those friendships to enrich and refine their character. Amen.

THOUGHTS ABOUT FRIENDSHIP

Love. It's a simple,

Love

four-letter word. . . .

*L*ove. It's a simple, four-letter word with huge, never-ending meaning. It communicates passionate emotions, loyal commitments, attitudes of the heart, actions of the will, and true motives.

If love were truly only what is pictured in romantic movies, we'd all be in trouble, for that kind of love is only a script. It isn't real—nor does it portray real love. True love shines in the trenches of daily life, when no one is watching. It changes diapers, scrubs a sink, rubs an aching stomach,

Kelsey, 7

and listens with a caring heart. Love is an attitude—and an action.

Sometimes, love means sharing a brief smile in passing, a knowing expression, or a helpful offer. Other times love is expressed through lengthy cheering sessions during a T-ball game, comforting hugs after a nightmare, and patient waiting while shoelaces are tied yet again. Love means sharing happiness and delight, but also sorrow and comfort. It believes in what is right, so it disciplines children for their own good. It believes that God will provide when money is scarce. It hopes for better times when health is poor or there's a relational struggle.

Love is so multifaceted that no single definition could ever do it justice. But the best definition of love is recorded in the Bible in 1 Corinthians 13:1-8: "If I could speak in any language in heaven or

on earth but didn't love others, I would only be making meaningless noise like a loud gong or a clanging cymbal. . . . Love is patient and kind. Love is not jealous or boastful or proud or rude. Love does not demand its own way. Love is not irritable, and it keeps no record of when it has been wronged. It is never glad about injustice but rejoices whenever the truth wins out. Love never gives up, never loses faith, is always hopeful, and endures through every circumstance. Love will last forever."

 Now *that's* the kind of love it will take a lifetime to fulfill.

May the Lord make your love grow and overflow to each other.

1 THESSALONIANS 3:12

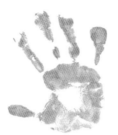

Activities with Children

1

Read a favorite story about love with a child or two. Talk about your favorite story

when you were young. Tell them how precious they are.

2

Stop a moment and marvel at the unique creation of the child in your life.

Of six billion people, you are looking at one of a kind.

Find a new way today to say, "You're special!"

Antics & Anecdotes

Love guides, leads, prepares, establishes.

Love [motivates us to] turn,

move or follow a straight course.

SARAH HORNSBY

put my picture here!

Love never gives up, never loses faith, is always hopeful,

and endures through every circumstance.

1 CORINTHIANS 13:7

After going through a battery of tests, an eight-year-old boy was asked by his family doctor if he would give his younger sister a blood transfusion that would hopefully save her life. She was critically ill with a disease from which he had recovered and for which he had developed antibodies.

The little boy considered the request for a few moments, and then he quietly agreed. He was subdued as the needle was inserted into his vein and his blood taken; but the physician and his parents were so focused on the seriously ill little sister in the next room that they paid little attention to his solemn mood.

Later, as the transfusion was completed, the boy called the doctor in to ask him a question. When the doctor heard the child's question, he wept. The eight-year-old boy wanted to know if he would have time to say good-bye to his family, or if he would die right away. Not understanding that the procedure was relatively harmless, the little boy believed that in giving his sister his blood, he was giving up his own life to save hers. He had been willing to die for her, to give up everything, because he loved her.

Anna, 5

Adapted from *"A BROTHER LIKE THAT"* *by C. Roy Angell*

many years ago a college friend of mine named Paul received a new automobile from his brother as a pre-Christmas present. On Christmas Eve, when Paul came out of his office, a street kid was walking around the shiny new car, admiring it. "Is this your car, mister?" he asked.

Paul nodded. "My brother gave it to me for Christmas."

The boy looked astounded. "You mean your brother gave it to you, and it didn't cost you nothing? Boy, I wish . . ."

He hesitated, and Paul knew what he was going to wish. He was going to wish he had a brother like that. But what the boy said jarred Paul all the way down to

Cara, 8

his heels. "I wish," the boy went on, "that I could be a brother like that."

Paul looked at the boy in astonishment, then impulsively asked, "Would you like to ride in my automobile?"

"Oh yes! I'd love that!"

After a short ride the boy turned, and with his eyes aglow said, "Mister, would you mind driving in front of my house?"

Paul smiled a little. He thought he knew what the boy wanted. He wanted to show his neighbors that he could ride in a big automobile.

But Paul was wrong again.

"Will you stop right where those two steps are?" the boy asked.

He ran up the steps. Then, in a little while, Paul heard him coming back, but he was not coming fast.

He was carrying his little polio-crippled brother. He sat him down on the bottom step, then sort of squeezed up against him and pointed to the car.

"There she is, Buddy, just like I told you upstairs. His brother gave it to him for Christmas, and it didn't cost him a cent. And someday I'm gonna give you one just like it. Then you can see for yourself all the pretty things in the Christmas windows that I've been trying to tell you about."

Paul got out and lifted the little child to the front seat of his car.

Gracie, 7

The shining-eyed older brother climbed in beside him, and the three of them began a memorable holiday ride.

That Christmas Eve Paul learned what Jesus meant when He said: "There is more happiness in giving than receiving."

Your children must know that your love is forever,

whenever, and with no strings attached.

MARY LA GRAND BOUMA

Emily, 5

Thoughts and Prayers

The person who hears the words "I love you!" from a child receives one of life's greatest gifts. May you be blessed by a child's spontaneous, unconditional love and encouraged to pass it on!

PRAYER

Heavenly Father, please grant this child the gift of love. Teach him what your unconditional love offers. Keep him close to you, and grow in him the desire and the will to care for others with that same love. Amen.

THOUGHTS ABOUT LOVE

Life is a process of

Learning Together

learning together. . . .

When you were a child, you learned your ABCs. But you also learned a lot of other things—like how to tie your shoes, to get along with your classmates, and to obey your mom when she asked you to put dirty clothes into the hamper.

Often we think of learning as only what happens through books and in the classroom. But learning extends past a spelling test to the affirmation of hearing your teacher say, "You did well." It moves past soccer game skills into the sportsmanship modeled following a referee's faulty call. Learning together involves both mind *and* heart.

Thankfully, no one person wears the instructor's cap at all times. For instance, parents teach their children

Kelsey, 7

that raking leaves together can be fun and that reading books makes for imaginative adventures. Children teach parents that mistakes are a part of growth and that hugs do help a boo-boo heal more quickly.

Life is a process of learning together, no matter what our age or stage. As we answer countless "Why?" queries from children, in the process we discover that some questions just don't have answers. And as our children increase their vocabulary, they discover that certain feelings cannot be expressed with words.

Many of life's significant lessons are learned in simple settings—

Kelly, 8

through a fireside chat or a visit to a park where leaves are falling from a tree. Even the removal of training wheels or the baking of chocolate-chip cookies can provide opportunities for great conversations. Jesus used gardens, hillsides, and seashores to teach his disciples some of their most profound life lessons.

Homes, schoolrooms, day-care centers, grandparents' houses—all are academies at which we can learn together. And if we pursue our life lessons with patience, love, kindness, and joy, we are providing children with a wonderful model to pass on to *their* children and grandchildren.

Keep these commandments carefully in mind. Tie them to your hand. . . .

Teach them to your children. Talk about them when you are sitting at home,

when you are out walking, at bedtime, and before breakfast!

Write them upon the doors of your houses and upon your gates.

DEUTERONOMY 11:18-20, TLB

Activities with Children

1

Talk about healthy foods and foods that aren't so nutritious. Prepare a meal together that

includes the four food groups: meat, dairy, vegetables and fruits, and grains.

2

Talk about a different country once a month. Find the country on a globe.

Read facts about it from an encyclopedia. Talk about how it differs from

our country and what it might be like to live there.

Antics & Anecdotes

Integrity is the glue that holds our
way of life together. What our young
people want to see in their elders
is integrity, honesty, truthfulness, and faith. . . .
Let them see us doing
what we would like them to do.

BILLY GRAHAM

put my picture here!

Teach your children to choose the right path,

and when they are older, they will remain upon it.

PROVERBS 22:6

God sends children for another purpose than merely to keep up the race—
to enlarge our hearts; and to make us unselfish and full of kindly sympathies and
affections; to give our souls higher aims; to call out all our faculties to extended enter-
prise and exertion; and to bring round our firesides bright faces, happy smiles, and
tender, loving hearts. My soul blesses the great Father every day,
that He has gladdened the earth with little children.

MARY HOWITT

Thoughts and Prayers

"Teachable moments" occur countless times a day. From putting the cap back on the toothpaste to looking both ways before crossing the street, learning very often takes place without any preparation.

PRAYER

Lord, help the children I know to be enthusiastic learners. Please give them a sense of wonder that lasts throughout life. Help them learn not only book knowledge but life skills that will protect and enrich their lives. Amen.

THOUGHTS ABOUT LEARNING TOGETHER

Memories can be both

Memories

bitter and sweet. . . .

†hink back to the first time a special child arrived in your life. Maybe it was through a thirty-hour labor or a teenage girl who entrusted her baby to you to raise. Maybe it was the first home where you became a nanny, the first time you became a grandparent, aunt or uncle, teacher, or leader of a children's group.

On this wonderful occasion, anticipation, fear, excitement, and joy probably all juggled for space in your heart. As you looked at the child or your group of children, you felt a deep awe for God's creative ability. Maybe you took lots of pictures and wrote down stories to help you recall memorable moments in later times.

Taneisha, 7

Children have an amazing ability to record themselves permanently on our hearts. And they're also inquisitive about your memories. "Grandpa, tell me again about the time Daddy got punished for climbing out his window!" "Tell me again, Aunt Sarah, where you met Uncle Doug." "Sing that song your grandma taught you when you couldn't sleep, Daddy."

Memories can be both bitter and sweet. They recall both life and death. They reveal both strength and weakness. But as they weave together the threads of the past, they add purpose to the present and inspire the tapestry of the future. Memories are not only for the aged to ponder in the comfort of a rocking chair—they are for everyone to share and pass on.

Memories are gifts from God that are waiting to be opened. So show those snapshots and journals, record those first haircuts and special Christmas tree ornaments, write down Grandma's molasses cookie recipe and Great-Uncle John's family joke. Tell stories, read letters, make and show videos, hang pictures of relatives. That's how life can go forward, touched for the better by the past. And even longer lasting than any photo or keepsake is the legacy of your character, values, and love—for these are the things that make memories.

Taneisha, 7

Christina, 11

147

I will praise you, my God and King.

Let each generation tell its children of your mighty acts.

PSALM 145:1, 4

Activities with Children

1

Let a child you spend time with pick one word.

Use that word to tell a story from your past.

2

Make a big bowl of popcorn and look at old family movies, photos, or slides.

Comment on some of your favorite memories together.

Antics & Anecdotes

FUNNY THINGS CHILDREN SAY AND DO . . .

Today is the last day of your
past and the first day of your future.
There's no better time than now
to begin "making memories"
with your precious family.

SHIRLEY DOBSON

put my picture here!

You saw me before I was born. Every day of my life was recorded in your book.

Every moment was laid out before a single day had passed.

PSALM 139:16

To John Leslie:

You were born one week ago tonight. And I've got to be honest, I'm not used to being a dad. I actually thought I had more time to prepare. Your mom and I have been praying for you long before you arrived, and now that you are here we know that God has given us a very special son.

Just two days ago as your mom and I moved our belongings home from the hospital, we were looking at the dozens of cards, flowers, and gifts from friends around the country and noticed a baby gift from God right out our front door. It was a remarkable, pristine rainbow. It was a sign of promise that God would be with us—and you—as you join our family. We named it "John's Rainbow." And I doubt we'll ever look at another rainbow without thinking of you.

As I write this letter, you are resting in an isolette at the neonatal unit in one of the finest hospitals on the West Coast. The tubes, monitors, lights, and alarms surrounding your bed don't phase you much, but the medical staff give them and you constant attention. Your entire body can fit in one of my hands, and my wedding band can easily slip over your entire arm and up to your shoulder. Your mother and I have spent many hours holding your head and feet, heeding the doctor's recommendation not to overstimulate you with too much rubbing and talking for now. We sing an occasional song and say short prayers. We'll have time for talking later.

Your grandfather, or Papa as he likes to be called, said a special prayer for you as he and I hovered over your tiny body this afternoon. You held on to one of my fingertips with surprising

strength as he asked God to empower the nurses and doctors who are helping you grow.

Papa, by the way, is the one who gave you your name.

John, you and I are just getting to know one another, but already, in a matter of days, I know I like you. You are a part of my family. You belong with me. The two of us go together. We have a lot to learn about each other, but one thing I know about you for sure: You like a challenge. The doctors tell us that only a very small percentage of babies

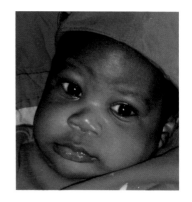

155

Chrissie, 7

your size enter the world the way you did. This very fact sets up a series of hurdles too numerous to mention, but in just seven days' time you're already working hard to overcome them.

Each day, as I study you from head to toe, I pause to watch your little chest move in and out, each breath synchronized with a meter that measures your oxygen. And each day your breathing has improved. Three days ago they examined your brain to find it functioning just the way it should. Your small eyes have opened a time or two to let us know you are alert. Your mother and I both know there will be setbacks, but I have a very strong feeling you are up for the challenge.

I love you so much, and I'm optimistic about your future. So before I close this letter I want to make a suggestion. When you are old enough, I want

you to visit a neonatology unit. I want you to see how far you've come. And if you are willing, I'd like to make that visit with you.

For right now, my dear son, I ask only that you rest. Tomorrow holds enough challenges for your tiny frame.

Your Daddy

Times have changed, and we can probably count on them continuing to change.
So it's up to us to seek out the little pieces of life that will become our children's memories.

SYLVIA HARNEY

158

Kelsey, 7

Thoughts and Prayers

Childhood memories are powerful and lasting, impacting our adult lives as well as future generations. What a privilege it is to be a part of creating happy memories for the children you know!

PRAYER

Lord, may the memories created today bring pleasure to the children in my life. Help them sift through the good and bad of life. Give them a deep peace and joy in knowing that they are blessed and held securely by you. Thank you for giving us the gift of remembering. Amen.

THOUGHTS ABOUT MEMORIES

Anisa Baker

Jim Bolton

Julie Chen

Tammy Faxel

Christina Fox

Kristin Gause

Mike Graham

Sharon Heggeland

Jeff and Linda Hoch

Carrie Jaruseski

Jeff Johnson

Mary Keeley

Donna Kelly

Barb Larson

Lucille Leonard

Kristen Mapstone

Kim Massey

John Mathes

Jackie Noe

Matt Price

Pushpa Ramgopal

Liz Rein

Marek Rossi

Lois Rusch

Peg Samuelson

Anne Steinbrecher

Robin Thompson

Sonja Thorson

Claudia Volkman

Linda Walz

Karen Watson

Pam Wiersma

Luann Yarrow